T0381108

GOD'S PLAN
and
PURPOSE
For YOU

LORETTA GIBELYOU

WESTBOW
PRESS®
A DIVISION OF THOMAS NELSON
& ZONDERVAN

This book is a work of non-fiction. Unless otherwise noted, the author and the publisher make no explicit guarantees as to the accuracy of the information contained in this book and in some cases, names of people and places have been altered to protect their privacy.

WestBow Press books may be ordered through booksellers or by contacting:

WestBow Press
A Division of Thomas Nelson & Zondervan
1663 Liberty Drive
Bloomington, IN 47403
www.westbowpress.com
844-714-3454

Because of the dynamic nature of the Internet, any web addresses or links contained in this book may have changed since publication and may no longer be valid. The views expressed in this work are solely those of the author and do not necessarily reflect the views of the publisher, and the publisher hereby disclaims any responsibility for them.

Any people depicted in stock imagery provided by Getty Images are models, and such images are being used for illustrative purposes only. Certain stock imagery © Getty Images.

Scripture quotations are taken from the King James Version, public domain.

ISBN: 979-8-3850-2764-4 (sc)
ISBN: 979-8-3850-2765-1 (e)

Library of Congress Control Number: 2024912195

Print information available on the last page.

WestBow Press rev. date: 07/10/2024

Testimonies

I had known about Jesus at the age of 8. I prayed and invited him into my heart at that time. I got baptized at the age of 12. Yes, Jesus came into my heart at the age of 8. It was exciting! All my siblings and my parents got saved, as well. We were very happy to receive and invite him into our lives.

- Barbara

I was saved and asked Jesus to forgive my sins and invited Him to come into my heart at age 7. I realized He died on the cross for my sins. I was then later baptized, making my confession of faith. God had always been with me through every up and every down in my life. I know in my heart He will never leave me or forsake me. I can hardly wait to see Him someday!!

- Laura

I gave my heart to Jesus when I was around 11 years old at a summer youth camp. The Youth Pastor led my friend, Sandy and I in the sinner's prayer, and we both asked Jesus in our hearts, and asked Him to forgive us all our sins. (I went to a mainstream church, but I had never been given the personal invitation to ask Jesus in my heart. ☺♥☺) I remember after I said the prayer of salvation, I felt so clean and brand new!! My friend, Sandy and I were both so excited! But I did not grow in my spiritual walk because I was never discipled in my Christian Walk. However, even as a teenager I did not feel the conviction of the Holy Spirit when I sinned. It was not until after my divorce and in college did I rededicate myself to Jesus and make Him Lord of my life. I was also baptized again as a symbol of my birth in Christ Jesus. (I was baptized as an infant, but this meant more to me.) It was a symbol of my new birth in Christ, picking up my cross and following Jesus. ☺!☺!♥!♥!♥!

- Mari Jo

To my Lord and Savior, forever and ever, my Grandmother, Loretta Teel, deceased, who showed me the way to Jesus! Tracy Parks, my cousin, for encouraging and inspiring me to publish this and my Pastor George H Wright, deceased, and the altar lady, whose name I don't remember, who led me through the sinner's prayer.

What is God's Plan and Purpose for You?

Everyone wanting to enter the kingdom of heaven must understand what is required. The following will help you, or those you know, accept the gift of salvation that is freely offered. The following is my personal experience.

God Loves You! 😄

God loves you! God loves you so much that He sent His only begotten Son, Jesus to save you so that you may enter His kingdom.

Read John 3:16, 17, 18 KJV

For God so loved the world, that he gave his only begotten Son, that whosoever believeth in him should not perish, but have everlasting life. For God sent not his Son into the world to condemn the world; but that the world through him might be saved. He that believeth on Him is not condemned: but he that believeth not is condemned already, because he hath not believed in the name of the only begotten Son of God.

Read John 3:36 KJV
He that believeth on the Son hath everlasting life: and he that believeth not the Son shall not see life; but the wrath of God abideth on him.

Read John 5:24 KJV
Verily, Verily, I say unto you, He that heareth my word, and believeth on him that sent me, hath everlasting life, and shall not come into condemnation; but is passed from death unto life.

Read John 6:40 KJV
And this is the will of him that sent me,
that everyone which seeth the Son, and
believeth on him, may have everlasting
life: and I will raise him up at the
last day.

Read John 6:47 KJV
Verily, verily, I say unto you, He that believeth of me hath everlasting life.

Read John 6:48 KJV
I am that bread of life.

Read John 8:51 KJV
Verily, verily, I say unto you, if a man keep my saying, he shall never see death.

(Note: of course will we be seeing physical death, but it is talking about eternal death).

Read John 3:36 KJV
He that believeth on the Son has everlasting life: and he that believe not the Son shall not see life; but the wrath of God abideth on him.

You receive your salvation when you sincerely believe and receive and invite Jesus into your heart and accept Him as Lord and Savior, and King.

God's purpose for His only begotten Son, Jesus Christ, to die on the Cross for us was not to bring condemnation, but to bring us, who pray and receive and invite Him into our heart, to reconciliation with God. He wants you to be saved (as in the prayer below)! To believe in Jesus Christ is to receive and invite Him into our hearts and ask Him to be our Lord, Our King, and Savior. <u>Remember: believe and receive and invite – even the devils believe and tremble. I believed for many years before I invited him into my heart</u>! I grew up learning about Jesus being the only begotten Son of God, that it was required of me to repent with a sorrowful heart and a sincere heart. I felt the calling of the Holy Spirit many times, but I did not go forward because I was so young I did not know I was supposed to go forward. After that I was too shy to go forward! After that I heard my pastor tell about the suffering He went through for me and then I went forward. You see, I believed for many years before I actually received and invited Him into my heart.

Read James 2:19 KJV
Thou believeth that there is one God; thou doest well: the devils also believeth, and tremble.

Read Matthew 21:22 KJV
And all things, whatsoever ye shall ask in prayer, believing, ye shall receive.

Read Mark 11:24 KJV
Therefore I say unto you, What things soever ye desire, when ye pray, believe that ye receive them, and ye shall have them.

Do you <u>Really</u> Need Jesus ? ? ? ?

The Verdict: The Whole World Stands Guilty before God. Yes, the Whole World!! Pray now and receive and invite Him into your heart to be your personal Lord and Savior!

Read Roman 3:10 KJV
As it is written. There is none righteous,
no not one.

Read Romans 3:23 KJV
For all have sinned and come short of
the Glory of God.

Yes! Yes! Yes! Yes! We **ALL** need Jesus!

Read Roman 6:23 KJV
For the wages of sin is death; but the gift of God is eternal life through Jesus Christ our Lord.

Eternal Death = Eternal Hell
Eternal Life   = Eternal Heaven

Which would you choose?

I accepted the sacrifice He did for me!

Hallelujah! Amen!!

Yes, we need him now –
we cannot save ourselves!

Read Matt 7:14 KJV
Because strait is the gate, and narrow
is the way, which leadeth unto life, and
few there be that find it.

We have found it!!!
It is Jesus, our Savior!!!

Can I get saved by good works?

Read Romans 3:10-12 KJV

10. As it is written, there is none righteous, no, not one: 11. There is none that understandeth, there is none that seeketh after God. 12. They are all gone out of the way, they are together become unprofitable; there is none that doeth good, no, not one.

No, you cannot be saved by good works, baptism, circumcision, confirmation, joining a church, giving money to the poor, giving money to the church, your best accomplishment(s), or other good works and deeds. You can't buy forgiveness or salvation. (When you receive salvation – it is a free gift to you, through the grace of God's Son, Jesus – it was purchased by His blood through His substitutionary death on the cross.) We must be a perfect man like our God to enter into Heaven, which we are not! And never will be!

Read John 1:12-13 KJV

But as many as received Him, to them gave he power to become the sons of God, even to them that believe on His name: Which were born, not of blood, nor of the will of the flesh, nor of the will of man but of God.

I am glad He gave us the power to become the children of God! Thank you, Lord. I give you all the power, all the glory and all the praise!

Read Ephesians 2:8-9 KJV.
For by grace are you saved through
faith; and that not of yourselves: it is
the Gift of God: not of works, lest any
man should boast.

What a wonderful, beautiful gift !! Thank you,
Lord!!

Is there another way to be saved?

No, there is not!

Read John 14:6 KJV
Jesus said unto him, "I am the Way, the
Truth, and the Life: no man cometh to
the Father, but by me".

He is The Only Way, the only Truth --there
is no other way! (We must go to him **directly**
through prayer to the Father.)

Open the Door!

Read Rev:3:20 KJV

Behold, I stand at the door, and knock: if any man hear my voice, and open the door, I will come in to him, and will sup with him, and he with me

Open up the door of your heart and invite Jesus in! Now, Now, Now!!

Salvation & Acceptance Prayer!
(Pray out Loud)

Dear Lord God, Heavenly Father,

I believe that Jesus is your only begotten Son, that He came from heaven to earth to die on the cross to save me from the penalty of my sin, and to give me **Eternal Life**. I believe that He was Resurrected from the dead on the third day and ascended into Heaven. *Lord Jesus, I am sorry for going my own way, I repent of my sinful life. I open the door of my heart and I invite you to come into my heart and be my Lord, my Savior and my King. **I thank you! In Jesus Name, Amen***

More Prayers

Heavenly Father, be King over every area of my life: my soul, spirit, mind, body, family, relationships, finances, and any other area of my life. In Jesus Precious Name. Amen.

Heavenly Father, free me from every area of bondage and hindrance I may have in my life including anger, fear, doubt, addiction, evil thoughts, witchcraft, false religions, negativity, profanity, insecurity, depression, low self esteem, unforgiveness towards You, others & myself, rebellion, violence, sickness, curses, poverty, misunderstandings, and misconceptions about You.

Be with me everyday. Help me to look to you for all things so that I can walk victoriously, resist temptations and overcome my past and any obstacles I will face in the future. Transform me into a mighty soldier in Your Kingdom.

Thank you! In the Precious <u>Name of Jesus</u>, Amen! Bless your Holy Name! I give you all the praise, honor, and glory!

True Christianity Provides a Savior

True Christianity is the only "religion" that provides a **Savior.** All other religions are based on works, traditions, behavior, good deeds or whatever rules they set up for you to follow. You are accepted if you live up to those standards and are condemned if you don't. No savior is provided.

False Christianity places the burden of Salvation on you.

In the positive, for the better part, it encourages better behavior and better citizenship in its followers (but <u>not</u> good enough to get into Heaven). In the negative it causes judgment, condemnation, criticism, comparing one another, etc. It can also be used to manipulate and control. False Christianity refuses to <u>receive</u>, <u>believe</u> and <u>invite</u> Jesus as Savior into our hearts. Good works cannot save! Salvation is a Gift from God.

The Burden of Salvation is Provided by God's Son, Jesus

The burden of salvation is provided because God sent His only Begotten Son, Jesus, to the World to be the Sacrificial Lamb who died on the cross to take away our sins. No other "religion" has provided a Savior. We can count on Jesus, our Savior! Religion being a bunch of rules for us to follow and <u>relationship</u> being a real experience we all can relate to.

Read I Peter 2:24 KJV
Who His own self bare our sins in His own body on the tree, that we, being dead to sins, should live unto righteousness; by whose stripes you were healed.

Read Romans 10: 3-4 KJV
For they, being ignorant of God's righteousness, and going about to establish their own righteousness, have not submitted themselves unto the righteousness of God. For Christ is the end of the law for righteousness to everyone that believeth.

We are now under Grace and not under the law <u>for those</u> who have <u>believed</u> and <u>received and invited</u> Jesus as personal Lord and Savior. If you have not received – then you are still "under the law". Choose <u>today</u> to receive Forgiveness and Grace! Now is the time! Now is **<u>YOUR</u>** moment!!

Read Roman 10:10
***For with the heart man believes unto
righteousness; and with the mouth
confession is made to salvation.***

(See Salvation and Acceptance prayer above).
(personal note: to *accept and agree* is made unto
salvation.)

Believing and Receiving/ inviting is a course of action!

Repent and invite Jesus into your heart to be Your Savior! I believed as a child but received and invited Him into my heart later when I was an adult. You can still believe and accept and invite as a child.

Yes, we know that "in your heart" is not in the Bible in those words, specifically, but I think we know what it means, even a child can know what this means. It means you! Your inner being, your soul, your spirit! Your spirit heart!

You Shall know the truth and the
truth will make you free!

"JESUS IS IN MY HEART"

To receive Jesus in my Heart means to choose one:

☐ Have love feelings in my heart for Him.

☐ I know something about Him from reading the Bible.

☐ I got baptized in water.

☐ I joined the church.

☐ I gave money to the church and to the poor.

☐ I was "confirmed". (Without receiving and inviting him in)

☐ I received communion this morning.

☐ I was circumcised.

☐ I go to church all the time.

☐ I do nice things for people.

- [ ] I am kind, loving and thoughtful to everyone.

- [ ] I do good deeds for people.

- [ ] I don't lie, steal, cheat, smoke, drink or do drugs.

- [ ] I never sinned, committed adultery or fornication, physically or spiritually.

- [ ] I have read the Bible all the way through 16 times.

- [ ] I repented because I know I am a person with a sin nature. I know I have "missed the mark" and can not earn my own way into Heaven. I realize that Jesus died for *my* sins on the cross for me and because I Invited Him into my heart to be *my* personal Lord, King, and Savior, He gives me Eternal Life. (He is Eternal Life). Jesus, the Holy Spirit, changes my spirit (regeneration) and then comes to live in my temple (my body).

The correct answer, of course, you know is the last answer. All the other answers are good answers, except you would deceive yourself if you thought you never sinned or that any other accomplishment other than the sacrifice God provided would "buy us a ticket" to Heaven. We try to live up to the perfection of God's standards, but we know we can't. The Lord God has understood our human weaknesses, and He provided His only begotten Son for us. I am grateful for God's Love and the obedience of Jesus, His Son.

Choose <u>Eternal Life</u> or
<u>Choose Eternal Death</u> !

☐ I chose the Gift of Eternal Life through Jesus.

☐ Go back and reread this and I hope you choose Jesus.

✝

Heaven rejoices when one sinner comes to the Lord ! Can you hear the angels singing?

To everyone who reads this
book, I hope you understand and
acknowledge that Jesus Christ is
the Son of the Living God, that we
need to repent, believe, receive/
invite Him into our hearts!

TO GOD BE THE GLORY,
HONOR, AND PRAISE!!

Why Am I Writing this?

Shortly after I repented, got saved and received and invited Jesus in my heart, I began hearing in my spirit the words of the ENEMY. He would say things like this and more:

You are not saved – just look at you! You can't be Saved! You are not good enough to be saved!

Look at this person in your family! You are not good enough to be saved!
Look at this person in your family! You all are not good enough to be saved!!
You people are just not good enough to be saved!

By the way – All three of us plus many others got saved! Praise the Lord! Glory to the Lord!

I would get up from my desk at work and go to the bathroom to pray several times a day because these evil thoughts bombarding me really disturbed me. This lasted for several months, maybe a couple of years.

This is the reason I started writing these things down. It gave me strength and resolve in my faith. The enemy was trying his best to cause me to doubt my faith. You can see it only helped me to continually go to Jesus. I started writing this for my own benefit. I did not think about writing a book early on, but my cousin, Tracy Parks, encouraged and inspired me to do this.

After being saved, I committed sin, some intentional, some unintentional and some so embarrassing that I would not mention. I remembered to go to I John 1:8,9 KJV and reread that. We will never be as good as God is no matter how hard we try and that is what is required to go to heaven, but Jesus dying his substitutional death, taking our sins upon him took care of that!

Read 1 John 1:8 KJV
If we say that we have no sin, we deceive
ourselves, and the truth is not in us.

Read 1 John 1:9 KJV
If we confess our sins, he is faithful
and just to forgive us our sins, and to
cleanse us from all unrighteousness.

Read 1 John 1:10 KJV
If we say that we have not sinned, we make him a liar, and his word is not in us.

I am not a pastor or a preacher, but I studied diligently for two to four hours a day for a long time just on the salvation issues. This is my story, and I am sticking to it!

All glory, honor and praise belong to Jesus!!

INVITE HIM INTO YOUR HEART TODAY!!

On November 3, 1974, I felt like I was bad because I had been divorced. I thought I deserved to go to hell. I was raised in church due to my grandmother's influence. I had decided to take my daughter, to church so she would not go to hell. A friend of mine at work, Alberteen, invited me to go to her church. I went and the Pastor told us about the suffering Jesus took on the cross for my sins. My heart was broken because of the things that they did to Him on that cross and I repented in sorrow because I was a sinner and He died for me. I went forward with the altar lady, and invited Jesus into my heart to be my Lord and Savior. Wow! Guess what? He came into my heart to stay, and I became born again! I was so happy! I wanted to tell everybody! I want to share with you to repent, believe, and receive/invite Jesus into your heart like I did to be your Lord and Savior. Invite him in <u>TODAY!</u> Before it is too late for you. <u>Now</u> is your time – before it is too late – don't wait on the rapture – we are not guaranteed another day.

Prayer:

Dear Lord God, Heavenly Father,

I believe that Jesus is your only begotten Son, that He came from heaven to earth to die on the cross to save me from the penalty of my sin, and to give me Eternal Life. I believe that He was Resurrected from the dead on the third day and ascended into Heaven. *Lord Jesus, I am sorry for going my own way, I repent of my sinful life. I open the door and I invite you to come into my heart and be my Lord, my Savior, and my King. I thank you, In Jesus Name, Amen.*

Note: If I sin again I will remember (Read: 1 John 1:8-10 KJV):

8. If we say we have no sin, we deceive ourselves, and the truth is not in us.

9. IF we confess our sins, He is faithful and just to forgive our sins and to cleanse us from all unrighteousness.

10. If we say we have not sinned, we make Him a liar and His Word is not in us.

========================

Yes! Yes! Yes!
I am Saved! Saved! Saved!
I am freed from
the penalty of my sins!

========================

I know that Jesus is the Savior of the World!

John 3:16 KJV:
For God so loved the world, that he gave
His only begotten Son, that whosoever,

_____

(Your name goes above)

believeth in Him should not perish but
have everlasting life.

Romans 5:8:
But God commendeth His love toward
us, in that, while we were sinners,
Christ died for us.

I know that Jesus came from Heaven to Earth
to die for me and to take the punishment of

my sins for me! He took my place for me! He died with my sins all on Him! After three days then He were resurrected into Heaven! He is the only Way, the only Truth, and the only Life. (Read John 14:6)

♡ What a Savior!! ♡

Saved on:

_____

Where:

_____

Baptized on : (obedience, and symbolic)

_____

Thank You, Jesus!

Our Family Legacy

Our Legacy starts with my great grandfather. The story has been told by my grandmother of him walking to work along the railroad tracks to the sulfur plant where he worked. He felt led to get on his knees and pray for Jesus to come into his heart.

My grandmother was next. I do not know her story, but I know her witness.

When I was a child, she came over on Sunday morning, got my sister and I out of bed, got us cleaned up, dressed us and took us to church with her. I admire her dedication to the Lord! I am so thankful to her for my experience. Many people in our family came to invite Jesus into their hearts thanks to her.

Inviting Jesus into your heart is your "ticket" to Heaven!

Jesus in your heart is your "ticket" to Heaven !!!

I have my ticket! Get Yours Today!

Printed in the United States
by Baker & Taylor Publisher Services